DRUGS & CONSEQUENCES

THE TRUTH ABOUT
COCAINE

TAMRA B. ORR

ROSEN
PUBLISHING®

New York

Published in 2014 by The Rosen Publishing Group, Inc.
29 East 21st Street, New York, NY 10010

Copyright © 2014 by The Rosen Publishing Group, Inc.

First Edition

Library of Congress Cataloging-in-Publication Data

Orr, Tamra.
The truth about cocaine/Tamra B. Orr.—First edition.
    pages cm.—(Drugs & consequences)
Includes bibliographical references and index.
ISBN 978-1-4777-1897-1 (library binding)
1. Cocaine—Health aspects—Juvenile literature. 2. Cocaine—Juvenile literature. 3. Cocaine abuse—Juvenile literature. I. Title.
RC568.C6O77 2013
616.86'47—dc23
                                                                    2013017782

Manufactured in the United States of America

CPSIA Compliance Information: Batch #W14YA: For further information, contact Rosen Publishing, New York, New York, at 1-800-237-9932.

CONTENTS

INTRODUCTION

You already know, as a teenager, that your brain is constantly busy. You are always juggling the details of class assignments, work schedules, and extracurricular demands. At the same time, you are responding to messages on Facebook and Twitter, downloading your favorite music on iTunes, and writing your latest blog post. Your life is full, busy, and occasionally a little crazy.

Although you aren't aware of it, your brain is changing as you juggle all of those tasks. For the first years of your life, that lump of gray matter inside your skull was developing at an astounding rate. Just think how much you learned between birth and kindergarten! While today's computers are amazing—and getting more and more sophisticated in what they are capable of doing—they are nothing compared to the speed and complexity of the human brain.

As you emerge into young adulthood, that enormous growth rate slows down as the mature brain you're going to lug around in your head for the rest of your life becomes more fully formed. That shift from youth to adult is a critical time, and if drugs like cocaine are introduced during this period, you—and your brain—can be in for some real trouble.

Although it may look like an innocent pile of white powder, cocaine is nothing but trouble from the start.

When it comes to cocaine, there is both good news and bad news. The good news is that cocaine use among young people is dropping. After hitting a high in the mid-1980s and experiencing a revival in the early 2000s, it has dropped to its lowest rates in years. According to national studies, 1.6 percent of eighth graders have tried cocaine, as well as 2.2 percent of sophomores and 2.7 percent of seniors. Too many young people are still experimenting with cocaine, but these numbers represent a significant decrease.

The bad news? Cocaine damages the teenage brain more than anyone thought. A recent Yale University study has shown that when adolescent brains are exposed to cocaine, the actual shape of the brain's neurons and synapses change shape in an attempt to protect themselves from the drug. The damage that cocaine does to young brains has been demonstrated in a number of studies. The University of Cambridge scanned sixty regular cocaine users and discovered that all of them had abnormal brains because of drug use.

What was different about their brains? The longer they had used cocaine, the less gray matter they had inside their skulls. The loss of this important part of the brain is connected with the overwhelming, obsessive need many users feel to keep taking the drug.

New information about cocaine and the teenage brain is coming out all the time, but some cold, stark facts aren't likely to change. Cocaine is dangerous, expensive, and addictive. It ruins lives, it destroys families, and it can kill you.

CHAPTER 1

THE LONG HISTORY
OF THE
COCA LEAF

When you look at the coca leaf, it certainly doesn't look dangerous. It looks like every other type of bush and plant found in tropical climates. The plant has flourished throughout South America for centuries. It grows best in warm, moist climates, usually on the side of hills and other high elevations. The plant can grow as tall as 8 feet (2.4 meters) and produces three harvests a year for many years.

Native South Americans have picked the coca leaf for hundreds of years, never dreaming it would one day be in high demand throughout the world.

The coca leaf is long and oval. It has played a huge part in South American history. There is evidence that these leaves have been used as far back as 3000 BCE. The leaves are actually quite nutritional as they are high in protein, vitamins, calcium, iron, and fiber. However, they also contain between .1 and .9 percent cocaine.

The First Energy Product

In the past, the coca leaf was used to make a paste. The leaf was rolled into a ball and then mixed with some seriously unappetizing-sounding ingredients, such as ground rock, sea-shells, ashes, and spit, and then tucked between the person's cheek and gum. There it sat, a lump in the cheek that was not chewed. Juices from the paste and the person's saliva would trickle down the throat for hours.

Historians have found that the coca plant was sacred to Incan royalty. Only the nobility, priests, and shamans were

This ancient figure from Colombia is depicted with a clump of cocaine paste stuck in his cheek for an all-day energy boost.

allowed to use it. They believed the plant was a gift from the sun god Inti and moon mother Moma Quilla. Coca was used for everything from treating the sick or wounded to playing a role in young men's initiation rites. It was even given to people right before they were sacrificed in Incan rituals so that their souls would go to paradise. Messengers who were given the job of running nonstop to deliver important news to other groups of people living far away were often given nothing other than coca leaves to chew or use as a paste. No food, no water—just coca and a fast journey.

When the Spanish conquistadors conquered the Incan empire, they quickly discovered that slaves worked longer hours if they were given plentiful amounts of coca leaves. In fact, the workers kept going without water or food as long as they had their leaves.

A Perfect Cure-All

By the middle of the nineteenth century, word about this wonderful plant that gave people extra energy reached Europe and North America. While the idea of mashing up the leaves and adding shells, rocks, or ash and then tucking it inside your cheek understandably didn't appeal to many people, they did like the idea of turning the leaves into a drink. In 1863, a chemist concocted Vin Mariani, a mix of wine and cocaine. It was advertised as a cure for pain, as well as an appetite suppressant and treatment for anemia.

This poster, produced more than a century ago, advertises the supposed health benefits of wine mixed with a dash of cocaine.

Advertisements of the time declare that the wine, which was 17 percent alcohol, "Nourishes, Fortifies, Refreshes, Aids Digestion, Strengthens the System."

In 1885, John Stith Pemberton heard about the interesting leaves. He had spent years marketing his health products such as Triplex Liver Pills and Globe of Flower Cough Syrup. He made a product he called French Coca Wine. Later, he replaced the alcohol with soda water and sold gallons of it to people looking for cures for depression and insomnia (which is odd, given cocaine's stimulating properties).

Another big fan of coca leaves as medical treatment was the famous psychoanalyst Sigmund Freud. He often prescribed coca as a cure for depression. "If all goes well," he wrote in a letter to his future wife, "I will write an essay on it, and I expect it will win its place in therapeutics by the side of morphine and superior to it . . . I take very small doses of it regularly against depression and against indigestion and with the most brilliant of success" (as quoted by Caleb Hellerman for CNN Health). By 1896, Freud realized he was probably addicted to the drug and managed to quit.

Other famous people, including inventor Thomas Edison and actor Sarah Bernhardt, used cocaine-derived products. Since such famous, accomplished, and influential people used them, the general public quickly followed suit. People of all ages consumed cocaine-based drinks. They were even given to children as a cure for toothaches. According to historian Howard Markel, "There were all sorts of health claims being made. If you had a stomach ache, if you were nervous, if you needed energy, if you had tuberculosis, if you had asthma, all sorts of things. It was going to cure what you had. And this was how it was advertised, too. Not only by marketers who made these drinks, but by major pharmaceutical houses."

An End to Elixirs

For almost fifty years, the presence of cocaine in wines, medications, and popular beverages was common. Movie stars were drinking these concoctions, doctors were prescribing them, and even military heroes and government leaders used them for extra energy. Some of these people even appeared in testimonials in newspapers throughout the country.

OPEN HAPPINESS?

You've heard the slogans: "Catch the Wave," "Life Begins Here," and "Open Happiness." Coca-Cola has had many catchy slogans over the years, and it remains one of the top-selling sodas in the world. In fact, Coca-Cola states that 1.8 billion Cokes are served every day across the planet. Some experts have criticized Coca-Cola for its high amounts of sugar and caffeine. However, if they had analyzed the formula when it was first invented in 1886, they would have had a lot more to complain about.

John Stith Pemberton was the first to create this new drink. He prescribed it as a "brain tonic and intellectual beverage." The original Coca-Cola contained about 60 milligrams of cocaine. Its original slogans were "Drink Coca-Cola" and "Delicious and Refreshing!" People definitely felt better after drinking it. It became a popular drink and sold for only five cents a glass. It was considered a healthy beverage. Even President Abraham Lincoln bought some in hopes it would help him grow a thicker beard.

This ad from 1906 appeared in *Scientific American* magazine, reminding everyone how wonderful cocaine-infused Coca-Cola was—and why consumers needed it.

By the end of the nineteenth century, suspicions about the effects of cocaine were on the rise. When the Pure Food and Drug Act was passed in 1906, all cocaine had to be removed from products. Does that mean that Coca-Cola stopped using the coca leaf to make its soda? Not quite. In the late 1980s, Coca-Cola officials admitted, "Ingredients from the coca leaf are used, but there is no cocaine in it, and it is all tightly overseen by regulatory authorities."

In the early 1900s, however, some people had growing suspicions that this amazing energy drink might be trouble. People who used it often seemed to quit drinking fluids, eating, and sleeping. Worse, they began to hallucinate and become somewhat delusional, seeing things that weren't there. The term "dope fiend" was coined to describe the person who continuously swung between being a raging ball of energy to a desperate, depressed person willing to do almost anything to get more of the drug.

By 1903, there was a passionate public outcry against any product containing cocaine. Pemberton had no choice but to take the coca out of his soda. He replaced it with much higher levels of caffeine. In 1906, the Pure Food and Drug Act was passed, requiring all of those mysterious potions and elixirs to be labeled with specific ingredients and their quantities. Immediately, the number of medications containing drugs like cocaine was reduced by one-third. By 1920, cocaine had been added to the growing list of narcotics banned under the Dangerous Drug Act that had been passed that year. Tragically, by then a number of people were already addicted, and no law was going to get in the way of them finding the next dose.

Drug of the Rich

For years, cocaine was not used by a large number of people and was not considered hip or fashionable. All of that changed in the late 1970s. "To be a cocaine user in 1979 was to be rich, trendy, and fashionable," says Mark Kleiman, coauthor of *Drugs and Drug Policy: What Everyone Needs to Know.* "People weren't worried about cocaine. It didn't seem to be a real problem." Cocaine made it possible for those with enough spending money to party all night and not need to take a break, get a drink, or eat any food.

When the well-known began dying from cocaine overdoses, however, people began paying more attention. Over the years, cocaine has been involved in the deaths of such celebrities as basketball star Len Bias, comedian Chris Farley, singer Whitney Houston, and actor River Phoenix.

Lawmakers responded quickly and harshly, setting up strict mandatory sentencing laws. Arrests skyrocketed, and the inmate population exploded, creating prison overcrowding problems across the country. Since then, the number of people using cocaine has dropped, a trend that everyone hopes will continue.

MYTHS & FACTS

MYTH It takes a long time and repeated use to get hooked on cocaine.

FACT Some people can become physically and psychologically dependent after only a few uses.

MYTH Cocaine does not have any side effects.

FACT Cocaine does have a number of side effects, including tremors, convulsions, infection, heart attack, stroke, psychosis, and even death.

MYTH You can develop an immunity to cocaine.

FACT You can build up a tolerance so that more cocaine is needed, but no one is immune to the drug itself.

CHAPTER 2

FROM PLANT TO DRUG

How does the long, oval coca leaf become the drug that people snort, inhale, or inject? It is a startlingly long and involved process. The plants, which grow best in higher elevations and cooler climates, have many leaves. These leaves are stripped from the plant and taken to a processing lab. Some of these illegal labs use acid to create the cocaine, while others use metal drums and gasoline.

Cooking Coke

Typically, the cocaine-making process goes like this. First, the leaves are soaked in gasoline inside metal drums. This pulls the cocaine alkaloid from the leaves. Next, the alkaloid is drained from the drums and filtered into a barrel with diluted acid. The gasoline is removed, and ammonia is added to create the cocaine base. This base is filtered through a cloth and dried to a thick powder.

The next step is dissolving this powder into a solvent, such as acetone or ether. This mix is heated to boiling. Then another solvent is added, along with hydrochloric acid. This causes the mix to crystallize. Any excess solvents are removed by hand and then again by a hydraulic press. Any possible remaining solvent is removed by putting the mix into a microwave oven. At this point, powder cocaine has been produced.

To make crack cocaine, the base is created by dissolving the cocaine hydrochloride into a mixture of water and baking soda. It is boiled until the cocaine element turns oily and sinks to the bottom of the container. Once excess water and other impurities are removed, the rocklike substance left behind is crack cocaine.

Snorting and Injecting

When you picture cocaine, you most likely imagine a pile of white powder. That is the most common way the drug has

Unexpected inspections of illegal cocaine laboratories throughout South American jungles are often led by armed soldiers.

been used. Powder cocaine is a water-soluble hydrochloride salt and is usually snorted. Using a straw or a rolled-up piece of paper, users lean over a line of cocaine and inhale through their nose, one side at a time.

The mucous membranes in the nose, as well as the sinuses, absorb the drug quickly. But only about 30 to 40 percent of the cocaine actually reaches the bloodstream and the brain. This

People snort cocaine with materials that are easily available.

type of cocaine can also be injected. The rush only lasts thirty minutes or less, unless the powder has been cut with other drugs as well.

Freebasing

Freebasing is another way that users ingest cocaine. Instead of snorting the cocaine, this technique involves smoking it. When freebasing, users heat and vaporize the cocaine and then inhale

COCAINE ON THE BREATH

For many years, police officers have relied on breathalyzers to determine if drivers have had too much alcohol to be behind the wheel. In Sweden, a new device has been created that can do even more than that. The Swedish breathalyzer appears to be able to detect a dozen different controlled substances, including meth (methamphetamine), heroin, morphine, marijuana, and cocaine.

This device was tested in a drug addiction emergency clinic in Sweden and was able to correctly identify drug use 87 percent of the time. This is as accurate as blood and urine tests—plus much faster and easier. Olof Beck, head of the study published in the *Journal of Breath Research*, stated, "In cases of suspected driving under the influence of drugs, blood samples could be taken in parallel with breath when back at a police station."

the smoke. The high from freebasing is often far more intense, although it lasts only a few short minutes. It is also one of the most addictive and dangerous methods of using cocaine.

Crack Cocaine

Crack cocaine, unlike ordinary cocaine, is a relatively new form of the drug. It was first introduced in the late 1970s and early 1980s. Crack is simply a solid form of cocaine. It looks

Crack cocaine is difficult to locate and confiscate because it can be hidden in many different containers, such as vials like these.

like an off-white nugget with sharp, rough edges. Its appearance is somewhat like a piece of candle wax.

Crack was first put on the streets by drug dealers because the cost of cocaine had dropped significantly. Rocks of cocaine could be broken into small pieces and sold for a much higher profit. Between 1984 and 1990, the country was hit with a crack "epidemic." The drug spread throughout the entire country and across the rest of the world.

To use crack, it has to be heated, usually in a glass pipe. The resulting vapors are inhaled. As the drug heats up, it crackles and pops, earning its nickname. The high from crack is the most intense and immediate, but also the shortest. It reaches the brain much quicker, and it often takes only one hit for a crack user to become addicted.

Whatever form cocaine is used in, it is devastating to both the brain and the body. It is an expensive, dangerous habit that trades a few minutes of a powerful high for serious side effects that can last a lifetime or even end a life. It is a risk that no one should take.

3

THE
COCAINE
RUSH

The power that cocaine has over those who use it is clear. From the "dope fiends" of the past to today's addicts, cocaine has driven people of all ages to do almost anything they can to get another fix. They are willing to use all of their money to pay for coke. They are willing to steal the money as well. Why does cocaine have this horrendous hold over users?

When you use cocaine, you feel a rush almost immediately. Your heartbeat revs up, as does your blood pressure and

While the high of cocaine may make you feel fantastic, the crash at the end is far worse. Even the high is not always pleasant for everyone. Many users experience panic and extreme anxiety during the so-called high.

breathing. Your pupils dilate and blood vessels constrict. Emotionally you experience what is known as euphoria. This means you feel wonderful, ecstatic, and absolutely invincible. You have the confidence to do anything, and you feel like you are "on top of the world." To others, however, you may appear restless, talkative, arrogant, and far too energetic.

Cocaine affects people in different ways, of course, and not all of them are necessarily pleasant. While a rush of happiness is typical, others may experience anxiety, panic, paranoia, tremors, vertigo, and muscle twitches. Some people even become violent. They may experience hallucinations in which they imagine bugs, snakes, or other creepy crawlies burrowing under their skin.

Up the Nose

The effect that cocaine has on the body largely depends on how the drug is ingested and what entry point it passes through. For the user who snorts the drug, the entrance point is obviously the nose.

Snorting cocaine is hard on the nose. The nose has a lot of important jobs. It brings in oxygen, warming and moistening the air as it does. It filters out dust, dirt, pollen, and germs through the mucous and the fine hairs, or cilia, lining the nostril walls. Of course, the nose is also responsible for smelling.

James Brown, pictured here, is a Scottish millionaire who used so much cocaine that his nose collapsed and his heart was severely damaged. On top of all this, he was also sentenced to prison.

Your sense of smell is extremely important. It keeps you safe by alerting you to potentially poisonous or toxic substances. On the other hand, it also reminds you that the chocolate chip cookies baking in the oven smell amazing, and they taste even better. Remember—most of your taste comes through your nose, not your tongue. That's why food tastes so bland and boring when you have a cold.

When you snort coke, the first thing that happens is that your nose goes somewhat numb because cocaine works like an anesthetic. This numbness can become a problem with repeated cocaine use because your nose can be seriously damaged, and with reduced sensation, you won't even be aware of it. Cocaine irritates your sinuses, so you feel congested at first, and then your nose starts to run like when you have a cold. Later, your nose will dry out inside, making it crack and bleed.

If you snort enough coke, your nose can become terribly damaged. Besides the cracking and bleeding, the drug can also eat a hole in your septum, the bone separating your nostrils. This can result in emergency surgery. In addition, snorting coke can destroy your sense of smell entirely. Food will not taste nearly as wonderful after that.

In the Veins

Injecting cocaine is preferred by some users because it tends to increase the intensity and duration of the high. Of course, taking coke in this way, just like injecting any drug, comes with a huge list of potential risks. Needles can be contaminated and expose you to possible diseases like HIV/AIDS and hepatitis B and C, as well as pneumonia and tuberculosis.

Multiple injections can irritate your veins and introduce infection. Your veins can eventually scar so much that they close up. When that happens, blood cannot flow properly, and you lose feeling and function in affected parts of the body.

THE GATEWAY SEQUENCE

If you've ever heard of the term "gateway drug," you know that many experts believe using one drug, such as marijuana, leads to using another, and then another. Although this idea is considered controversial, a 2011 study helped establish the connection.

Researchers found that people who smoked cigarettes were more apt to try cocaine and end up addicted to it. The experiment conducted by the Columbia University Medical Center discovered that the nicotine found in tobacco causes the brain to change and become much more vulnerable to drug addiction. Under certain circumstances, smoking dramatically enhances a person's response to cocaine for reasons still being investigated.

The next question is whether other gateway drugs also increase the brain's vulnerability to cocaine addiction. So do alcohol and marijuana—the two most common gateway drugs—prime the brain for addiction in the same way as nicotine? That question is sure to be explored in future experiments.

In the Lungs

Inhaling and smoking cocaine damages your lungs. It can even make them bleed. Smoking cocaine can also cause chest pain and breathing difficulties. Being so close to the flames that heat the drug can result in burns to the skin, eyebrows, and eyelashes.

In the Heart and Brain

Cocaine acts like a direct jump-start to your heart. Under the influence of cocaine, your heartbeat speeds up so much that it can disturb the normal rhythm. Cocaine also raises your blood pressure, putting you at higher risk of heart attacks and strokes. In a recent Australian study, researchers found that recreational cocaine users have higher blood pressure, stiffer arteries, and thicker heart muscle walls than nonusers. All of these elements can trigger a heart attack. Dr. Gemma Figtree, leader of a Sydney Medical School study, reports, "We are repeatedly seeing young—otherwise fit—individuals suffering massive heart attacks related to cocaine use. Despite being well-educated professionals, they have no knowledge of the health consequences of regularly using cocaine. It's the perfect heart attack drug."

At the same time, the brain is severely impacted by cocaine, which can induce strokes, seizures, headaches, and even coma. The majority of cocaine-related deaths are due to either cardiac arrest or the seizures associated with respiratory arrest.

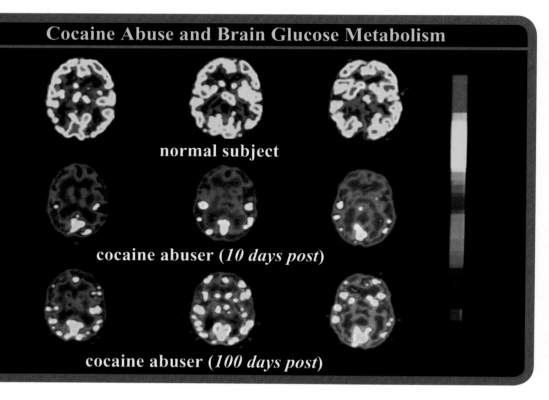

Cocaine Abuse and Brain Glucose Metabolism

normal subject

cocaine abuser (*10 days post*)

cocaine abuser (*100 days post*)

These images show the differences between normal brains and those of short- and long-term cocaine users.

The physical devastation of cocaine use does not end there. Continued use can damage your liver and kidneys. It can cause your teeth to decay and fall out. It can make sex difficult and threaten your ability to eventually have children.

The Effects of Crack

Does crack cocaine have different effects on the body than cocaine? It carries all the same risks as coke, along with a few

OUT ON THE STREET

Cocaine goes by many different names on the street. They are constantly changing and even vary from one part of the country to the next. Here are some of the most common nicknames:

- coke
- snow
- blow
- cola
- rock
- crack
- rails
- nose candy
- toot
- white
- coco puff
- powder
- fluff
- sniff
- bad rock
- bazooka
- beam
- Bernice
- big C
- blast
- blizzard

additional ones. Crack is often mixed with ingredients that can send out toxic fumes when burned. Crack pipes are very short,

The cycle of cocaine abuse often results in anger, depression, illness, alienation, and isolation.

and it is very easy to burn your lips when inhaling, resulting in a condition known among users as "crack lip." Because crack is typically inhaled, long-term use can also result in coughing, shortness of breath, and respiratory failure.

DEALING
WITH
ADDICTION

f you had the chance to ask a dozen people who were
addicted to cocaine what their goal was in taking the drug,
not one would say to get hooked, spend all of their money,
damage their bodies, or injure their brains. Chances are
their reasons would range from wanting to have a good time
or giving in to peer pressure to satisfying curiosity, relieving
stress, or just escaping from regular life. It is likely that every
single addict would love to go back in time and never take that
first hit of coke.

Cocaine use, abuse, and addiction can change every part of your life and lead you down a pathway that ends in misery.

With cocaine, many people get hooked psychologically first and physically second. The rush you get from cocaine—those minutes of total euphoria—can be incredibly pleasurable. Can you think of a time in your life when you felt extremely happy? When everything in the world seemed to be going your way and you were capable of anything you set your mind to? Cocaine often brings you those feelings times ten. When you experience a high like that, coming back down to earth can be depressing and upsetting. Where did that feeling of invincibility go?

How does cocaine manage to make you feel both so invincible and so miserable? To understand this, you need to understand how the drug impacts the different parts of your brain.

Stimulating Pleasure Centers and Disrupting Brain Chemistry

When a person snorts, inhales, or injects cocaine, the drug goes right to the ventral tegmental area (VTA) of the brain. This is a small area at the base of your brain, just underneath the hippocampus. The VTA is where the pleasure centers of the brain are found. When you're having an amazing day and catch yourself singing in the shower and walking around with a big smile on your face, it is because this area is being stimulated. It might be the result of having a great time with friends, eating the best cheeseburger you've ever tasted, acing a really difficult test, or receiving an unexpected compliment that meant a great deal to you.

What you aren't aware of is that when you're having a stellar day, it is because a chemical called dopamine is being released in your brain. A special transporter circulates the dopamine so that, eventually, your extreme happiness eases off a bit because nature knows that too much of a good thing is often simply too much. When a person takes cocaine, however, that transporter is blocked, so the dopamine keeps building up, making you feel better and better and better.

Your brain, however, is a flexible organ. As you keep taking cocaine, it adapts to the drug. You begin to build up a

SHINING A LIGHT ON ADDICTION

Can you cause or cure addiction with nothing more than a laser? A study from the National Institutes of Health (NIH) thinks it just might be possible. NIH researchers have determined that they can get rid of addictive behavior in rats using a laser to stimulate a specific part of the brain known as the prelimbic region in the prefrontal cortex. Using the laser on rats that are not addicted to drugs, on the other hand, can create a sudden craving for drugs. Researchers believe that this study may hold hope for people that are addicted to serious drugs like cocaine. Instead of using lasers, however, scientists would use a technique called electromagnetic stimulation on a person's scalp.

tolerance to it. This means you need to take more coke more often to achieve the same rush you used to get. Thus begins one of those awful, endless cycles. You take coke, feel great, and then, when it wears off, you come back down to normal. Normal doesn't feel very good anymore, though. In fact, now you're struggling with crushing depression. Life seems boring and bland. Hanging out with friends, watching a great movie, playing your favorite video game—none of these once-beloved activities seems like much fun anymore.

This is largely due to the fact that cocaine damages how your brain produces dopamine. Before the coke, your brain produced just the right amount, at the right times, to help you feel happy. Now, however, because the coke has been interfering with dopamine production, your ability to feel good and experience pleasure fades when you aren't taking the drug anymore.

The memory of how cocaine made you feel compels you to get more coke and consume it again in order to regain those emotions. The drive can become a compulsion. Even if you have sincerely promised your parents, your friends, and yourself that you are done with coke, the thought of the euphoria you once experienced can result in huge cravings worse than anything you've ever experienced. It makes your old midnight munchies for buttered popcorn and pepperoni pizza seem like nothing.

The drive to obtain and ingest more coke can make a normally logical person do irrational things. You may find yourself using your college savings account to buy coke. You might sell your bicycle or cell phone for extra money. You might steal money from your family and friends. You might rob a store. You might offer sexual services in return for cash. Anything to get the money you need to feel happy again.

In addition to interfering with your dopamine production, cocaine also disturbs your brain's production of the chemical neurotransmitters serotonin and norepinephrine. Serotonin controls your internal clock, letting you know when you need to eat and sleep. Norepinephrine is the chemical involved in your "fight or flight" response, which kicks in

COCAINE ANONYMOUS

In late 1982, in Hollywood, California, the first Cocaine Anonymous (CA) meeting was held. The organization was founded to provide a fellowship for recovering addicts. Based on the same twelve steps of the Alcoholics Anonymous (AA) organization, CA states that it is designed for "men and women who share their experience, strength, and hope with each other that they may solve their common problem and help others recover from their addiction. "

The group only requires that members want to stop using cocaine. There are no dues or fees to pay. "Our primary purpose is to stay free from cocaine and all other mind-altering substances, and to help others achieve the same freedom," states the organization's Web site. Meetings are held in every state in the United States, as well as in Canada and Europe. Currently, CA has more than thirty thousand members.

when you are faced with an emergency. Cocaine does not allow these neurotransmitters to move through and be recycled. Instead, they build up. When this happens, your cues that it is time to eat, drink, or sleep are blocked. You have what feels like endless energy. You are almost vibrating with pent-up drive to go, do, move!

Conversely, when the cocaine wears off, and dopamine, serotonin, and norepinephrine all return to normal levels, the user is left feeling depressed and exhausted. He or she is often suffering from malnutrition and dehydration because of a lack of food and water. The high may have been good, but when it ends, it is guaranteed that you are going to face serious problems.

Additional Dangers

If the damage done to your emotions, mind, body, and rela-tionships isn't enough, cocaine also exposes you to many other problems. First, the powder form of cocaine is often cut, or mixed with, other materials that are not good for the body either. Common ingredients include household prod-ucts like sugar, cornstarch, baking soda, and baby powder. Some dealers also lace their cocaine with methamphet-amine, or "meth." This makes the rush of cocaine much stronger—and much more dangerous. Meth is a very potent drug that is easy and cheap for the seller to make but potentially lethal for someone to use.

Using cocaine increases the chance of contracting other serious illnesses such as HIV/AIDS and hepatitis B and C. The risk comes from sharing contaminated needles and drug paraphernalia, such as straws and glass pipes. Users also become vulnerable to disease by participating in risky behaviors associated with cocaine use and addiction. These can include risky sexual encounters or trading sex for drugs or drug money.

Using cocaine carries additional dangers to what is actually in the powder itself. People under the influence of

Everyday people are sent to prison for using and possessing cocaine. The man pictured here was sentenced to sixteen months for possession of cocaine. Just a few months after he was released, he was arrested again during a domestic abuse call and found with three doses of crack cocaine at home.

cocaine often feel invincible and powerful. They take risks they would never take under normal circumstances. These can range from physical challenges, such as jumping off a roof or running into traffic, to criminal behavior, such as speeding and driving erratically. Some users even commit serious and violent crimes like robbery or assault.

The cause-and-effect relationship between drugs and criminal behavior is strong. In a recent survey of inmates in state and federal correctional facilities, 32 percent of state prisoners and 26 percent of federal prisoners were found to have committed their offenses while under the influence of drugs.

Warning Signs

If you are worried that one of your friends or someone you care about might be using cocaine, here are some of the most common physical signs to watch for:

- Regular nosebleeds
- Chronic runny nose
- Bloodshot, red eyes
- Dilated pupils
- Sensitivity to light
- Chills or hot flashes
- Burns on lips or fingers
- Hoarse voice
- Tracks or puncture marks
- Dramatic weight loss

Here are the most common psychological or behavioral changes to watch for:

- Personality changes
- Apathy
- Violent or impulsive behavior
- Frequently borrowing money
- Unexplained financial problems
- Changes in sleeping patterns
- Reduced eating and dramatic weight loss
- Overly talkative or energetic
- New set of friends
- Problems at work or school
- Periods of depression followed by excitability
- Periods of paranoia or panic attacks
- Insomnia
- Irritability
- Missing appointments, work, or school
- Stealing
- Lying
- Rapid speech

After looking at this list, if you suspect that someone you know might be using cocaine, what can you do about it? First, talk to a trusted adult in private about the situation. It can be your parents, a teacher, or a coach. You don't have to reveal your friend's name, but just ask for some advice and

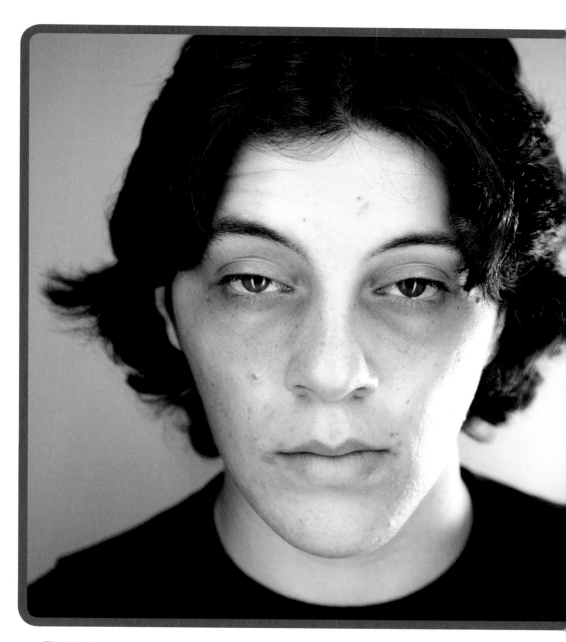

The look of someone who has been using cocaine is often a signal to friends and family that something is terribly wrong.

guidance. Second, talk to your friend. Don't do it when there are other people around or when he or she is high. Make sure you approach the topic as a concerned and caring friend, not an accusing or judgmental scold. Third, give specific reasons why you suspect your friend is using coke. Fourth, offer to help. Provide a list of local, state, or national addiction-related organizations, rehab centers, or hotlines that your friend can contact. Offer to drive your friend there or help him or her make the initial call. Finally, be prepared for the fact that your friend might get very angry and defensive when you talk to him or her. He or she might deny everything you're saying, but don't give up. Be there to listen and help if your friend opens up to the idea.

CHAPTER 5

TREATMENT AND RECOVERY

If cocaine gives you such an intense high, you can bet it also delivers an even more extreme low. What is it like to go through cocaine withdrawal? Unlike the withdrawal process from a number of other drugs, cocaine withdrawal is rarely accompanied by severe physical symptoms. There is no vomiting or shaking as with heroin or alcohol. There are no muscle aches and spasms or diarrhea. That does not mean it is easy, though.

Once the last coke binge is over and the high has worn off, the crash follows. Your neurotransmitters return to normal levels, and depression is not far behind. The crash brings intense cravings for more cocaine, and these cravings can be absolutely overwhelming. For many addicts, the only thing they can think about is how to get more cocaine, even if they had every intention of quitting.

In addition to cravings, withdrawal symptoms often include irritability, agitation and restlessness, fatigue, vivid dreams, and depression so severe that thoughts of suicide are not uncommon. An addict in withdrawal is likely to sit around not moving much, feeling no joy in life, having no motivation, and wanting little more than sleep.

Dealing with all of these emotions can be terribly difficult for the addict, even if he or she has the full support of family and friends. Many cocaine addicts have no choice but to enter some type of treatment center.

Dealing with Cocaine Addiction

Facing cocaine withdrawal is tough—so tough that it is virtually impossible to do without professional help. Most treatments focus on helping addicts deal with one thing: cravings. Without a doubt, it is the cravings that send people back for the next dose of coke.

At home, cravings can be managed with the help of a few techniques. These work well for some people, especially those who have not used coke for a long time. Some find help

Some cocaine users, like the woman pictured here, are sent to live in addiction recovery homes, where they are expected to remain clean and hold down a job.

through distraction. They find ways to keep themselves busy, rather than sitting at home idle, obsessing about cocaine and trying to figure out a way to get the next hit. Some possibilities include taking a walk, going to a movie, doing chores like grocery shopping, or going for a bike ride.

It often helps people to focus on the reasons why they stopped using cocaine. They may even make a list, including such reasons as "I will lose my job if I keep using" and "My parents will take my car." Still others talk through their cravings, sharing their feelings and frustrations with a close friend. Voicing the experience can often help a person accept the emotions and move on.

It also helps to remember that cravings are like a wave. They build up, crest, and then subside again. Learning to ride the rise and fall of the cravings like a surfer on the ocean can make it easier to get through each wave of desire. Exercising can also be a great way to combat addiction and its cravings. Moving your body releases endorphins, which help anyone feel better and provides a natural and healthful "high."

A COCAINE VACCINE?

For several years, scientists have tried to create a vaccine that would block cocaine from reaching the brain and generating the euphoria that is so addictive. After all, if there is no high or rush, there will be no interest in the drug.

An antiaddiction treatment that would use our own bodies to fight off addiction is a relatively new idea in medical science, but a promising one. According to Ronald Crystal, a researcher at Weill Cornell Medical College in New York, "If the vaccine works, then it would block the cocaine from reaching the brain and they [users] wouldn't feel anything."

To date, the vaccine has worked well in monkeys and mice, but whether or not it will work in humans is questionable.

So far, the vaccine has not performed well in human testing. Researchers are still working to find just the right vaccine formula to immunize users against the addictive rush of cocaine.

Getting Professional Help

It is rare that a person can handle quitting cocaine without the expert assistance of a professional counselor or outpatient program or time spent in a treatment center. Although hotlines can be helpful, treatment centers tend to be more effective. These centers often follow different recovery programs, but most of them will include some of the same activities, including:

- Medical testing and evaluation
- Complete abstinence from the drug
- Group counseling
- Individual counseling
- Nutritional support
- A twelve-step program
- Sports and games
- Exercise programs
- Family programs

Some therapy programs also offer religious or spiritual counseling, art therapy, anger management classes, marriage counseling, meditation and relaxation workshops, stress management lessons, and relapse prevention classes.

One of the most common techniques used to treat cocaine addiction is the cognitive-behavioral approach. It begins by focusing on cravings. Counselors help users understand the withdrawal experience better and the associated cravings.

Communities in Schools is part of a substance abuse counseling program that helps kids get off drugs and do better in school.

Recovering addicts are encouraged to accept cravings as a normal part of recovery. Counselors also help people determine what triggers those desires. It might be spending time with a certain person, drinking alcohol, or having money in their pocket. Knowing these cues can help people either avoid these triggers or be extra careful and vigilant when exposed to them.

Therapists often spend time with addicts asking questions like, "What is a craving like for you?," "How bothered are you by the craving?," "How long does a craving last for you?," and "How do you try to cope with the craving?" They also help addicts cope with the overwhelming desire for a drug through distraction, discussion, acceptance, recollection, and self-talk.

Counselors in treatment centers teach patients ways to distract themselves. They also encourage them to talk about the

craving in order to help reduce the feelings of anxiety and dis-
tress when they think about it. Counselors reinforce the idea of
seeing the craving as a wave and experiencing each one without fighting it—or giving in to it. Instead, recovering addicts
need to ride the wave and know that it will crest and subside.
Next, therapists have addicts focus on the many negative consequences associated with cocaine use and addiction. Often
they recommend that patients write down these consequences
and carry the list in their wallets or purses as a constant
reminder.

Finally, treatment centers often employ the method of self-
talk with patients. Counselors know that many addicts have a
tendency to have automatic thoughts about cocaine that they
may not even be consciously aware of. These thoughts can
include, "If I don't get some coke, I'll die" or "I can't work/be
with people/go to school if I'm not using." Therapists help
patients confront those negative statements and replace them
with positive thoughts such as, "I will be fine without cocaine"
or "Cravings are normal and I can get through them."

Some drug addictions are treated by taking other drugs to
help the body detox and cope with the many withdrawal
symptoms. This is not true with cocaine, however. There are no
drugs that help patients cope, although some centers will pre-
scribe antidepressants and antianxiety drugs to help take the
edge off of the depression that many patients experience.

When looking into a rehab program, some of the most
important questions for a patient or a patient's family to ask are:

- What is the center's philosophy on addiction?
- Is the center accredited?
- What is the center's success rate?
- How long will it take to complete treatment?
- What services are covered by health insurance?

After Treatment Ends

Once treatment ends, does this mean a cocaine addict is cured? Not necessarily. Relapse is common, so many centers offer some type of aftercare. Usually aftercare programs include post-treatment monitoring, alumni support groups, and monthly check-ins with staff members.

Cocaine is one of the most powerful drugs anyone can take. Whether it is injected, inhaled, or snorted, it changes the user's body upon contact. It is a drug that can result in addiction with only one use, and those few minutes of euphoria come at a huge price. Cocaine costs you money, relationships, health, and possibly even a future. It opens you up to risks that you might spend the rest of your life paying for.

It took hundreds of years for people to figure out that the simple coca leaf was not so simple after all. That innocent-looking, long, oval piece of greenery growing high on the mountainsides of South America has caused disaster, devastation, and death for countless people all over the world. Don't let yourself be one of them.

TEN

1. Does using drugs like marijuana make it more likely that I will use something stronger, such as cocaine?

2. If I wanted to use cocaine only once to see what it was like, could it do any serious damage?

3. What are the differences between snorting, injecting, and smoking cocaine?

4. How does cocaine differ from crack cocaine?

5. Is it legal to use cocaine in any part of the United States?

6. Has the number of teens using cocaine gone up or down in recent years?

7. How does cocaine affect my brain and emotions? How does it affect my body?

8. How can you tell when you have become addicted to cocaine?

9. How does it affect the baby if a pregnant woman uses cocaine?

10. Why is cocaine considered one of the most addictive drugs available?

GLOSSARY

acetone A colorless, flammable liquid.

anemia A deficiency of red blood cells, resulting in exhaustion.

anesthetic A substance that produces numbness.

cilia Tiny hairs that line the surface of cells in the nose, lungs, and other locations within the body.

dilate To expand or make wider or larger.

dopamine A neurotransmitter associated with pleasure centers of the brain.

elixir A potion or drink often used for medical purposes.

endorphin A neurotransmitter associated with pain and the "fight or flight" response.

ether A flammable liquid used in the past as an anesthetic.

euphoria A state of intense happiness and self-confidence.

hippocampus A part of the brain that plays an important role in consolidation of information from short- and long-term memory and in spatial navigation.

hydraulic Operated or moved by water or liquids in motion.

methamphetamine A central nervous system stimulant, also known as meth.

narcotic A drug that blunts the senses and can cause hallucinations.

neuron An impulse-conducting cell in the nervous system.

neurotransmitter A chemical substance that transmits nerve impulses across a synapse.

norepinephrine A neurotransmitter that controls blood pressure.

paranoia A mental disorder characterized by the feeling that someone is chasing, following, or menacing you and intends to do you harm.

prefrontal cortex The anterior part of the frontal lobe of the brain involved in planning complex cognitive behavior, personality expression, decision making, and moderating social behavior.

prelimbic region A part of the brain that plays a role in the expression of fear.

respiratory arrest The cessation of breathing.

septum The bone between the nostrils in the nose.

serotonin A neurotransmitter associated with sleep, memory, and emotions.

shaman A priest or priestess who uses magic for the purpose of curing the sick, divining the hidden, and controlling events.

suppressant A substance that stops or decreases an action or condition.

synapse A region where nerve impulses are transmitted and received.

vertigo A sensation of dizziness.

FOR MORE INFORMATION

American Addiction Centers
115 East Park Drive, 2nd Floor
Brentwood, TN 37207
(877) 586-7128
Web site: http://www.americanaddictioncenters.com
American Addiction Centers offer help, sup-
    port, and guidance to addicts of all kinds.
    The Web site offers a live chat with a repre-
    sentative and resource materials for addicts,
    as well as for their loved ones and cowork-
    ers. A toll-free number is available for asking
    questions.

Canadian Center on Substance Abuse (CCSA)
75 Albert Street, Suite 500
Ottawa, ON K1P 5E7
Canada
(613) 235-4048
Web site: http://www.ccsa.ca
The CCSA is dedicated to reducing alcohol and
    drug-related harm. It provides access to a range
    of information and analysis relating to substance
    abuse issues and connects Canadians to a broad
    spectrum of networks and activities.

Co-Anon Family Groups World Services
P.O. Box 12722
Tucson, AZ 85732-2722
(800) 898-9985
Web site: http://www.co-anon.org
Co-Anon Family Groups is a fellowship of the husbands, wives,
    parents, relatives, and close friends of those addicted to
    cocaine. It offers helpful information, a newsletter, a group
    directory, meetings, and other resources.

Cocaine Anonymous World Services (CA)
21720 South Wilmington Avenue, Suite 304
Long Beach, CA 90810-1641
(310) 559-5833
Web site: http://www.ca.org
Cocaine Anonymous is a fellowship of men and women who
    share their experience with cocaine addiction. Its motto is
    "Hope, Faith, and Courage." Its Web site offers educational
    material, meeting details, and resource links. The site also
    has self-tests for addiction and offers details about CA's
    annual convention.

Council on Drug Abuse (CODA)
215 Spadina Avenue, Suite 120
Toronto, ON M5T 2C7
Canada

(416) 763-1491

Web site: http://www.drugabuse.ca

CODA is a nonprofit organization that sponsors preventive
alcohol and other drug education programs in schools for
students, teachers, and parents.

National Institute on Drug Abuse (NIDA)

6001 Executive Boulevard

Room 5213, MSC 9561

Bethesda, MD 20892-9561

(301) 443-1124

Web site: http://www.drugabuse.gov

NIDA focuses on the science behind drug abuse and addiction.
It provides specific materials to researchers, parents and
teachers, patients and families, medical and health professionals, and students and young adults.

Web Sites

Due to the changing nature of Internet links, Rosen Publishing
has developed an online list of Web sites related to the subject
of this book. This site is updated regularly. Please use this link to
access the list:

http://www.rosenlinks.com/DAC/Coca

FOR FURTHER READING

Bickerstaff, Linda. *Cocaine: Coke and the War on Drugs*. New York, NY: Rosen Publishing, 2009.

Brown, Sarah. *Cocaine* (Health Issues). Bel Air, CA: Hodder Wayland Children's Publisher, 2009.

Connolly, Sean. *Cocaine* (Straight Talking). Mankato, MN: Creative Company, 2009.

Gillard, Arthur. *Drug Abuse* (Issues That Concern You). Farmington Hills, MI: Greenhaven Press, 2013.

Hawkins, John B. *The Dirty, Nasty Truth: 18 True Crime Stories and 10 Life in Prison Stories to Stop Juvenile Delinquency*. Escondido, CA: Dark Planet Publishing, 2012.

Hecht, Alan, and David J. Triggle. *Cocaine and Crack* (Understanding Drugs). New York, NY: Chelsea House, 2011.

Keegan, Kyle, and Howard Moss. *Chasing the High: A Firsthand Account of One Young Person's Experience with Substance Abuse*. New York, NY: Oxford University Press, 2008.

Peterson, Savanna, and Jill A. Vanderwood. *Drugs Make You Un-Smarter*. Seattle, WA: CreateSpace Independent Publishing, 2011.

BIBLIOGRAPHY

Armunanto, Eko. "Laser Treatment on the Brain to Switch On/Off Cocaine Addiction." *Digital Journal,* April 10, 2013. Retrieved April 2013 (http://www.digitaljournal.com/article/347701).

Bayer, Linda. *Crack and Cocaine.* New York, NY: Chelsea House, 2000.

Chastain, Zachary. *Cocaine: The Rush to Destruction.* Broomall, PA: Mason Crest Publishers, 2008.

Coca-Cola.org. "Coca-Cola History." Retrieved April 2013 (http://www.worldofcoca-cola.com/coca-colahistory.htm).

Daily Mail. "Cocaine Is 'the Perfect Heart Attack Drug'—Even If You Only Use It a Few Times a Year." November 6, 2012. Retrieved April 2013 (http://www.dailymail.co.uk/health/article-2228582/Cocaine-perfect-heart-attack-drug--use-times-year.html).

Hathaway, Bill. "Cocaine and the Teen Brain: Yale Research Offers Insights into Addiction." *Yale News,* February 21, 2012. Retrieved April 2013 (http://news.yale.edu/2012/02/21/cocaine-and-teen-brain-yale-research-offers-insights-addiction).

Hellerman, Caleb. "Cocaine: The Evolution of the Once 'Wonder' Drug." CNN Health, July 22, 2011. Retrieved April 2013 (http://

www.cnn.com/2011/HEALTH/07/22/social.history
.cocaine/index.html).

Holmes, Ann. *Psychological Effects of Cocaine and Crack Addiction.*
New York, NY: Chelsea House, 1999.

Karberg, Jennifer C., and Christopher J. Mumola. "Drug Use and
Dependence, State and Federal Prisoners, 2004." Bureau
of Justice Statistics, October 11, 2006. Retrieved April 2013
(http://bjs.gov/index.cfm?ty=pbdetail&iid=778).

Koebler, Jason. "New Breathalyzer Can Detect Marijuana, Cocaine,
Heroin." *U.S. News & World Report,* April 25, 2013.
Retrieved April 2013 (http://www.usnews.com/news/articles
/2013/04/25/new-breathalyzer-can-detect-marijuana
-cocaine-heroin).

May, Clifford. "How Coca-Cola Obtains Its Coca." *New York Times,*
July 1, 1988. Retrieved April 2013 (http://www.nytimes.com/
1988/07/01/business/how-coca-cola-obtains-its-coca.html).

MonitoringtheFuture.org. "2012 Overview: Key Findings on
Adolescent Drug Use." 2012. Retrieved April 2013 (http://
www.monitoringthefuture.org/pubs/monographs/mtf
-overview2012.pdf).

National Institute on Drug Abuse. "A Cognitive-Behavioral
Approach: Treating Cocaine Addiction." Retrieved April 2013
(http://archives.drugabuse.gov/TXManuals/CBT/CBT8.html).

ScienceDaily.com. "Abnormal Brain Structure Linked to
Chronic Cocaine Abuse." June 22, 2011. Retrieved April
2013 (http://www.sciencedaily.com/releases/2011/06/
110621074342.htm).

ScienceDaily.com. "Cocaine and the Teen Brain: New Insights into Addiction." February 21, 2012. Retrieved April 2013 (http://www.sciencedaily.com/releases/2012/02/120221212616.htm).

ScienceDaily.com. "Nicotine Primes Brain for Cocaine Use: Molecular Basis of Gateway Sequence of Drug Use." November 2, 2011. Retrieved April 2013 (http://www.sciencedaily.com/releases/2011/11/111102190400.htm).

UCLA.edu. "Freud's Magical Drug." Retrieved April 2013 (http://www.botgard.ucla.edu/html/botanytextbooks/economicbotany/Erythroxylum).

Welsh, Jennifer. "How Cocaine Vaccines Could Cure Drug Addiction." Live Science, June 22, 2012. Retrieved April 2013 (http://www.livescience.com/21132-cocaine-vaccine-cure-addiction.html).

INDEX

About the Author

Tamra Orr is the author of numerous nonfiction books, including many related to science and health. She has a degree from Ball State University and lives in the Pacific Northwest with her husband and family. She loves to camp, read, write letters, and travel with her family. She reads the grossest details about drugs to her kids to make sure they never go anywhere near them.

Photo Credits

Cover, p. 1 photopixel/Shutterstock.com; pp. 4–5 Milos Jokic/E+/Getty Images; pp. 7, 17, 24, 33, 45, 54, 56, 59, 60, 63 Oleg Golovnev/Shutterstock.com; p. 8 Aizar Raldes/AFP/Getty Images; p. 9 DEA Picture Library/DeAgostini/Getty Images; p. 11 Buyenlarge/Archive Photos/Getty Images; p. 13 Fotosearch/Archive Photos/Getty Images; p. 19 AFP/Getty Images; p. 20 Wavebreak Media/Thinkstock; p. 22 Jodi Cobb/National Geographic Image Collection/Getty Images; pp. 25, 32 iStockphoto/Thinkstock; p. 26 Rex Features/AP Images; p. 30 NIDA/NIH; p. 34 Juanmonino/E+/Thinkstock; p. 40 © Earnie Grafton/The San Diego Union Tribune/ZUMA Press; p. 43 Oliver Ingrouille/E+/Getty Images; p. 47 © Fairbanks Daily News-Miner/ZUMA Press; p. 50 © AP Images.

Designer: Sam Zavieh; Photo Researcher: Amy Feinberg